School and Society
Who is Molding Whom?

By
Angel Freddy Medina Segura

Dedication

Welcome, teachers, pedagogues all those who seek to reinvent themselves every day with the purpose of giving the best and thus forging a better nation. This information is prescribed for all those who are part of the school system from its different spaces. The educational community has been the central axis of these reflections, so we have tried to contribute those fundamental ideas that give life to the school. We dedicate this writing to students, parents, guardians, teachers, and administrators of education.

With special attention to my fellow students, co-workers and the teachers who continue to forge us. To you, we try to delivery this material to receive these enriching criticisms. We leave this reflective analysis in your hands with the intention that this beginning motivates the curiosity to delve deeper into these issues.

Table Of Contents

Chapter 1: Where The Old School Was Left

Education is one of the fundamental pillars of any society. For centuries, the school has been the place where knowledge has been transmitted and new generations have been formed. However, in recent decades, the education system has undergone an unprecedented transformation. The school, as we knew it, has ceased to exist.

The traditional educational model, based on the memorization of data and the transmission of knowledge in a unidirectional way, has given way to a more flexible and adaptive model, which considers the individual needs and abilities of each student. The incorporation of recent technologies and globalization have radically changed the educational landscape, which has led to a series of challenges for education.

In this chapter, we will delve into the reflection on the evolution of the school and the educational system throughout history, to understand the changes and transformations that have taken place in recent years. We will analyze the latest trends and pedagogical approaches that are being developed with the aim of better understanding the current panorama and proposing solutions that guarantee quality education for all.

Particularities of the Old School

The old school as we know it is gone. Traditional education models based on data memorization and one-way transfer of knowledge do not meet the needs of today's society. Twenty-first century schools must adapt to new demands and social changes to produce critical, creative, and autonomous citizens.

It should be noted that the old school was characterized by a teaching based on discipline, authority, and respect for the figure of the teacher. However, at present, the educational model has evolved towards a more participatory and student-centered approach, which seeks to foster their critical and creative capacity.

In fact, the old school focused on the transmission of knowledge and technical skills. It was characterized in individual learning, while the new school seeks to encourage teamwork and collaboration among students. The old school focused on articulate and rote teaching, while the new school seeks to foster meaningful learning and the development of higher cognitive skills, such as creativity, critical thinking, and complex problem solving.

However, over time, the old school approach has been criticized for its rigidity and lack of flexibility. Proponents of the new school argue that education should be tailored to each student's individual needs and abilities and encourage creativity and critical thinking.

Jiménez (2007), from his book "Old Wardrobe" said there was no manual when he looked through the old files he references. Jiménez adds to his story: "Environment and School" (Communication), by Miguel Sánchez de Castro, is an interesting book, available only in limited edition. Dating from the 1930s, this book, like many others, marked a shift towards an initiative-taking and pragmatic methodology. But what he found in those lies and shadows, filled with the smell of pigeon nests that filled everything, convinced him that it was possible to create this collection of material. The author goes into detail describing how the school was accepted at the time.

The painting of Franco and José Antonio, with his hair covered in glitter, at first gave me a strange feeling, as if I were reopening one of those closed schools after fifteen years and colliding with the crucifix. Even though little time had passed, there had been a meaningful change. I woke up to find myself in a frozen time or as the main character of The Time Tunnel TV show. There were still dates, samples on those old blackboards, some of which were even painted on the wall, as well as figures of sticks and broken clouds that appeared when the chalk was removed. There were plaster images on tiny wooden bases, the school almanac nailed to the wall along with some old works, and faded maps with leaks in many classrooms in addition to the official iconography mentioned above (Jimenez, 2007).

Despite these criticisms, there are those who argue that the old school still has something to offer in terms of values and principles. In the old school, there was a great emphasis on discipline, challenging work, and personal responsibility. These values are considered by some to be fundamental to succeed in life and in the labor world.

In addition, the old school also valued respect for authority and tradition, as well as the importance of maintaining high ethical and moral standards. These values can be especially relevant in an increasingly complex and globalized world, where stability and social cohesion may depend on the adoption of common norms and values.

The old school focused on uniformity and standardization of knowledge, characterized by a formal, structured, and hierarchical education. In addition, it was characterized by a quantitative evaluation, based on examinations and numerical grades. To this, the figure of the teacher is added as the exclusive source of knowledge, while the new school seeks to promote informal learning and access to multiple sources of information and knowledge through ICT. The former educational model focused on the transmission of values and social norms, while the new school seeks to train critical citizens, capable of actively participating in the construction of a more just and equitable society.

There are many attempts to transform the school; the answers given about school change come from quite different concerns. Within the existing difficulties, the most relevant responses are gathered into three large groups that accentuate the dialectic, relational and sociopolitical aspects. In addition, the great shouts to the traditional school are framed, which are the inadequacy of the old school with modern life, the inefficiency it shows to make that adjustment, the divorce between school and life, not taking into account the personality of the student, his great authoritarianism, promotion of individualism instead of collaborative work and the fact that it has a merely social and political role (Jiménez & ESO 2009).

Vivero (2017) argues that the beginning of the digital era in Ecuador 23 years ago resulted in a continuous shift from traditional media to new ones. In addition to being forced to move online, media also had to adapt to the needs of a challenging demographic group, millennials. A generation that is used to using multiple screens and expects more new stories from the media.

Ferrari (2015) understands that, in twenty-first century schools, many of the traditions of the school are still in use. The difficulty many institutions face in adapting to new capabilities arising from interactive and connective media is evident in the delay involved in realizing that learning is achieved through the student's ability to focus on one task at a time. Similarly, exposing students to classroom and off-classroom learning environments that do not stimulate these deep-seated daily habits leads to maladjustment and exposes the fundamental issues teachers address when it comes to curriculum, topics, and classroom development.

It should be noted that the old school of teaching that focused on memorization and repetition has been largely left behind due to the evolution of education throughout the nineteenth, twentieth and twenty-first centuries. While this form of teaching was useful at the time in preparing the workforce in the industrial age, the focus on understanding, reasoning, and practical application of knowledge has proven to be more effective in preparing students for the current and future world.

Teaching methods have become more personalized, adapting to individual student´s needs, and novel approaches have been introduced, such as project-based learning and STEM education, which is the acronym for science, technology, engineering, and mathematics terms. In addition, technology has played a significant role in the evolution of education, enabling online teaching and distance learning.

In any case, although the old school of teaching has become obsolete, it is still important to recognize its place in the history of education and the contribution it made to the development of modern education. However, in today's ever-evolving world, it is necessary for teaching methods to continue to evolve to meet the changing needs of students and society at large.

The Evolution of Teaching Methods in the Course of History

Education has been an integral part of society since ancient times. Subsequently, teaching methods have evolved to meet the changing needs of education. In this section, we will explore the evolution of them throughout history, from ancient Greece to the modern era.

A multidimensional phenomenon, teaching has been the subject of study. Thus, a variety of analyses were deepened, including those dealing with sociology, symbols, ethnography, politics, and intersubjectivity. There were numerous studies of different themes or problems of the various teaching modalities. The investigations became extremely analytically weighted and at the same time extremely fragmented. As a counterpoint, the initiative-taking nature of the didactic intervention and its ability to develop fundamental standards and general guidelines that support teachers in making decisions when teaching was abandoned (Davini, 2008).

In other of his writings, Davini (2008) argues that the most significant changes involve conflicting processes rather than cumulative variations, which forces those associated with these disciplines to rethink the network of commitments that underpin their scientific practices. The analysis of extra-methodological factors, or ideological factors, in times of crisis and the transformation of thought and associated disciplinary practice within the expert community are two of the most fascinating features of these "revolutions".

These changes are nothing new in the field of educational sciences. However, as in a select few, from the expert community, they reflect a tendency towards fragmentation, in which it is often possible to observe attempts at domination, rather than the fusion of several actors of knowledge or the recomposition of postulates. In particular, the debate on didactics sometimes has disturbing edges. We frequently witness discussions about the segregation of territories rather than the productive exchange between disciplines and the spaces between them (Davini, 2008).

In ancient Greece, education was a privilege reserved for social elites. Students attended public and private schools to learn literature, music, philosophy, and sports. Education focused on the formation of the mind and body. Teaching methods based on memorization and repetition were used. Students memorized long passages of literature and philosophy and then recited them from memory. This teaching method was based on the idea that repetition was the key to retention and understanding.

Thus, the first myths promoting the idea of justice appeared in ancient Greece. Hesiod called it The Nightingale's Tale. Demetrius Faleroni was the author of the first historically attested collection of legends, but since then it has been published in several editions. If we talk about the fables of the famous writer Aesop, one of the most well-known is Augustana. In his collection, he refers to the most famous and important legends about children and youth. popular literature (Rodríguez, 2010).

In the Middle Ages, education focused on training priests and monks. Most schools were narrow and focused on teaching theology and philosophy. The teaching method is based on memorization and repetition. Students memorized and memorized long passages of the Bible. Memory was seen as the key to understanding and remembering.

The educational history of antiquity is inextricably linked to our contemporary culture. It serves as a reminder of the origin of our own pedagogical tradition. That relationship, which is reflected in our educational system, is determined by our Greco-Columbian culture. When the greatest Renaissance of the fifteenth and sixteenth centuries occurred, the modern idea of education was fixed by a return to the more rigid classical tradition. More often than we realize, we still rely on the humanist legacy today (Marrou, 2004).

During the Renaissance, education became a subject of general interest. Humanists believed that education should be available to everyone, not just social elites. The Renaissance was a time of discovery and advances in science and technology. New teaching methods were developed, such as the Socratic method, which focused on discussion and debate rather than memorization and repetition. This teaching technique was based on the idea that discussion and debate were the key to understanding and retention.

Socrates' approach consists of two parts: one that is destructive and the other that is creative. The interlocutor's conception of the issue at hand serves as a starting point for the first stage of Socrates' argument, which allows him to identify its flaws and contradictions. In the second stage, known as maieutic, Socrates imagines himself as a midwife who helps his interlocutor to give birth, discover and reveal the truth within him, as well as lift the veil that hides that truth. The Socratic method, which consists of pretending to be ignorant of the subject at hand in order to reveal the truth through dialogue between expert and apprentice, depends on the methodical application of irony (De la Torre, 2003).

Beginning in the seventeenth century, education focused on training political and military leaders. Teaching methods seem to be gone back in time. Students memorized long passages of history and literature and recited them from memory. Memorization was believed to be the key to understanding and retention.

Aguilar (1988) argues that, in Spain, without a predetermined plan and without a clear sense of the future, other subjects were added to the middle ground occupied by Latin grammar between primary and university education during the Enlightenment. Although it aims to modernize education, there is not enough political will to address the underlying social and economic issues that are driving these problems. The absolutist state issues directives and passes laws to support people who contribute financially and personally to educational reform.

During the eighteenth century, education became a subject of general interest. The Enlightenment philosophers believed that education should be available to everyone, not just social elites. New teaching methods were developed, such as the Montessori method, which focused on observation and experimentation rather than memorization and repetition. This teaching method was based on the idea that observation and experimentation were the key to understanding and retention.

During the nineteenth century, education became a subject of immense importance due to the emergence of the Industrial Revolution. Education focused on training the workforce, with an emphasis on reading, writing, and math. Teaching methods were based on rote memorization and repetition, but new methods were also introduced, such as the mutual teaching method, which involved students tutoring other students. Vocational and technical schools that focused on training for specific jobs were also developed.

Sauter (1993) argues that, after gaining independence, the model of the State that develops in Ibero-America quickly seizes educational authority to the detriment of the Church. This basis allows for the secularization of society, the affirmation of the nation-state, and the emergence of a middle class that sees education as an engine of social mobility. As the processes of industrialization and productive diversification advance, at the same time it contributes indirectly to economic progress.

During the twentieth century, education underwent a great deal of change. With the rise of learning theories and educational psychology, teaching methods focused on understanding, reasoning, and practical application of knowledge.

others teaching methods were introduced, such as the Montessori method and the Waldorf method, which focused on learning through exploration and play.

Technology was also introduced into education, enabling distance learning and online teaching. Television, educational programs, and online education became popular forms of teaching and learning. Education also focused on cultural diversity and inclusion, leading to the introduction of multilingual education programs and the teaching of the history and culture of different ethnic groups.

For Muñoz et al. (1999), the turn of the century and the millennium, characterized by both utopianism and skepticism, were exciting times for Western societies. It is exciting because people expect massive things to happen in their lives as we head into the legendary year 2000 and start a new century. There were also doubts that the next century would bring great discoveries that would affect science.

In the twenty-first century, education has continued to evolve, thanks to technological advances. The use of mobile devices, such as smartphones and tablets, has led to a change in the way people are taught and learned. Teaching methods have become more personalized, adapting to the individual needs of students. Project-based learning has been introduced, allowing students to work on programs that interest them and that allow them to apply knowledge in practical ways.

There has also been an increased emphasis on STEM (science, technology, engineering, and mathematics) education, which has led to the introduction of new ways of teaching and learning in these areas. Education has also focused on social and emotional knowledge, which aims to teach skills such as conflict resolution, empathy, and effective communication.

For Aguerrondo (2017), Today's democratic schools make the skills and morals necessary to contribute to a vibrant and supportive society accessible to all citizens of the country, regardless of socioeconomic status, race, or religion. Education also has an impact today because it plays two important roles in helping to meet the needs of tomorrow's society. Equality and inclusion are protected by education and competitiveness is protected by education.

Reform in education is a common response to changes in the economy, production methods and changes in the process of economic and cultural globalization in all latitudes. However, the results were different than expected. They find it difficult, if not impossible, to succeed, and this is their common trait (Aguerrondo, 2017).

Dramatic social, economic, and political changes over the past 40 years have rendered traditional schools obsolete, inefficient, and inappropriate. Not because it has always been this way, but because of the new demands and challenges that a changing society brings. This explains why there are huge differences between societies and education systems in almost every country in the world today. Traditional schools remain the most usual form of education in the world. This leads to a growing gap between schools and modern society. Contrary to widely held belief among Latin American educators, this distinction is not exclusive to Latin America (their region). This is because the changes described are consistent with a globalized world and traditional schools remain the dominant educational model even in developed countries (De Zubiría, 2019).

In short, the evolution of teaching methods throughout history has been wide and diverse. From traditional methods of memorization and repetition to modern and technological methods, the most effective way to transmit knowledge and skills to students has always been sought. Teaching methods have evolved to adapt to the needs of a changing society and the demands of the labor market, going from being a unidirectional process to an interactive one, where the student is the protagonist and center of the educational process.

It is worth noting that educational approaches are constantly evolving and adapting to meet the needs and challenges of contemporary education. Nowadays, technology plays a leading role in education, serving as an essential tool for learning. Pedagogical methods have become dynamic processes, where different technologies and methodologies are integrated to achieve meaningful and personalized learning. Finally, the evolution of educational approaches has been constant, and will continue to be so in order to meet the challenges of the current and future world.

The Relationship Between Education and Social and Economic Development

The relationship between education and social and economic development is fundamental in the development of a society. Education is an essential tool for achieving the economic and social progress of a country or region. Investment in education is a crucial step in reducing poverty, improving people's quality of life, and promoting equal opportunities. In addition, quality education can contribute to job creation, innovation, and sustainable economic growth.

In terms of social development, education can be seen as a determining factor in the formation of informed and participatory individuals. A quality education can help individuals develop social and emotional skills, such as empathy, collaboration, and respect. These skills (they) can foster a more equitable, just, and harmonious society. In addition, education can be a useful tool for promoting gender equality and combating discrimination and racism.

When it comes to the advancement of a country's or region's economic well-being, learning can be regarded as a driving force for productivity and progress. Quality knowledge can enhance the efficiency and effectiveness of workers, leading to greater productivity and reduced production expenses. Furthermore, education can serve as a wellspring of innovation and entrepreneurship. Educated individuals are more prone to establish innovative firms and play a role in developing new products and services.

Monroy and Flores (2009) state that, particularly if we consider the economic constraints that apply to developing nations, the contribution of human capital theory to national economic development is still unclear. Weakly integrated nations have fewer opportunities to develop their human capital because they treat education as a commodity. Despite harsh criticism, human capital theory remains steadfast in seeking logical solutions to these problems.

In another order, education can be seen as a principal factor in poverty reduction. It can provide individuals with the skills and knowledge needed to access better jobs and wages, which in turn can improve their quality of life and reduce deprivation. In addition, education can be a valuable tool for reducing social and economic inequality. Quality education can provide all individuals with the same opportunities and resources to develop their skills and talents.

For Ranis and Stewart (2002), the style of development is linked to the inability to offer meaningful employment to a rising number of workers and the susceptibility to changes in the global situation. Changes in the existing model of development will ultimately result in a stalemate or societal collapse due to the escalating income and lifestyle disparity and the increasing impoverishment of the majority. These alternatives can become too costly, unjust, and unrealistic over time. All of this is interconnected with productivity and citizenship education.

The relationship between education and social and economic development is necessary for the progress of a society. Education is a useful tool for achieving poverty reduction, equal opportunities, innovation, productivity, and sustainable economic growth. In addition, a quality education can foster important social and emotional skills and promote equity and social justice. Therefore, investment in education is a long-term asset that can significantly improve the social and economic development of a society.

Montenegro (2013) argues that, in theory, the connection between social mobility and inequality can be complicated. However, there is a direct connection between them in practice, according to some authors. The chief White House economic adviser under President Obama, Alan B. Gatsby, proposed the so-called Gatsby curve. According to Krueger, nations with high social mobility also have low inequality, as indicated by low Gini indices. On the other hand, societies with high inequality show little social mobility.

In relation to the above problem, education is a crucial factor in the social and economic development of any society. Education not only provides people with the knowledge and skills needed to succeed in life, but it also a means to foster equal opportunities, reduce poverty, and promote innovation and sustainable economic growth. This contracts with social mobility.

In terms of social development, education is fundamental in the formation of informed and participatory individuals in society. It enables people to understand and participate in the political process, which in turn can lead to a more just and equitable society. In addition, school can be a valuable tool for promoting gender equality and combating discrimination and racism. A quality pedagogy can foster important social and emotional skills, such as empathy, collaboration, and respect, which in turn can contribute to a more harmonious and cohesive society.

In terms of economic development, education can be seen as an engine for productivity and economic growth. Quality education can improve worker efficiency and effectiveness, which in turn increases productivity and reduces production costs. Furthermore, it can be an important source of innovation and entrepreneurship. Educated individuals are more likely to create innovative companies and contribute to the development of new products and services. In addition, a quality education can provide individuals with the skills and knowledge needed to access better jobs and wages, which in turn can improve their quality of life and reduce poverty.

It should be noted that, education also has a key role in promoting health and well-being. Schooling can be seen as a determining factor in preventing disease and promoting healthy lifestyles. Moreover, knowledge acquisition can help people understand and cope with mental health-related challenges, which in turn can contribute to a healthier and more productive society.

Within this same order of ideas, education is a key factor in the social and economic development of any society. Education not only provides people with the knowledge and skills needed to succeed in life, but is also a means to foster equal opportunities, reduce poverty, and promote innovation and sustainable economic growth. Investment in education is a long-term investment that can significantly improve the social and economic development of a society.

Education has a significant impact on the economic growth of any country. Countries with prominent levels of education tend to have stronger and more sustainable economies over time. This is because education fosters the development of skills and competencies necessary for innovation, productivity, and competitiveness. Salas (1997), citing Gómez (1981), argues that education has been thought to be vital to increase human productivity by allowing people to participate in the labor market in better circumstances and, subsequently, earn more money to live better. Due to the importance given to "educational credentials" as a means of prestige and social mobility, it has generated social pressure for educators.

An educated workforce is critical to the economic growth and prosperity of any country. People with quality education are more likely to get better paid jobs, which in turn can improve their quality of life and reduce poverty. In addition, an educated workforce can be more productive, as it has the skills and knowledge needed to cope with the ever-evolving challenges of the labor market.

Education is also a key driver of innovation and entrepreneurship. Educated individuals are more likely to create innovative companies and contribute to the development of new products and services. In addition, education can be seen as an important source of knowledge and skills needed to access new sectors and emerging markets.

On the other hand, education can also have an impact on the distribution of wealth and the reduction of economic inequality. Individuals with quality education are more likely to have access to better jobs and wages, which in turn can reduce the income gap and improve the quality of life of the general population.

Besides, education can be a determining factor in reducing poverty and improving the health and well-being of the population. People with quality education are more likely to understand and cope with challenges related to health and well-being, which in turn can contribute to a healthier and more productive society.

In short, education is a key factor in the economic growth of any country. It fosters the development of skills and competencies necessary for innovation, productivity, and competitiveness. Moreover, education can improve the distribution of wealth, reduce economic inequality, and improve the quality of life of the population. Investment in education is a long-term asset that can have a significant impact on the economic growth and prosperity of any society.

Education is a powerful tool for achieving social equity and mobility in a society. Education gives individuals the opportunity to gain the skills, knowledge and experience needed to succeed in life and advance their career. In addition, education can play a vital role in reducing the income gap and promoting social justice.

First, education can be a tool to break the cycle of poverty. Low-income people are less likely to have access to quality education, which can prevent them from acquiring the skills and knowledge needed to find a well-paid job. By providing quality education to low-income youth, they are given the opportunity to break the cycle of poverty and improve their quality of life.

Education can serve as a means to achieve equal opportunities. Individuals from various socioeconomic backgrounds may have uneven access to educational opportunities, resulting in disparities in their personal and professional lives. All individuals, irrespective of their social status, can have the chance to compete fairly in the labor market and society, when they receive equitable access to education.

Schooling has the potential to promote gender equality and dismantle obstacles to inclusion. Women and girls frequently confront cultural and financial obstructions to obtaining education, which can restrict their chances in life. Women and girls can compete on a level playing field in both the labor market and society as a whole, if they receive equal access to education.

Undoubtedly, education is a powerful tool to achieve social equity and mobility in a society. Pedagogy can break the cycle of poverty, be a tool for equal opportunities, improve social mobility and have an impact on gender equality and the removal of barriers to inclusion. Asset in education is a long-term investment that can have a significant impact on equity and social justice.

However, although the relationship between education and social and economic development is positive, there are a number of features that can affect this connection in diverse ways. Below are some of the main factors (ones) that can influence it:

1. Level of investment in education: Investment in education is a key factor for social and economic development. While increased education funding has been shown to have a positive impact on economic growth and social equity, governments often face budget constraints that limit their ability to spend on education.

2. Quality of education: It is also a principal factor that can influence the relationship between education and social and economic development. While access to education is mandatory, the educational attainment is equally important. If education is not of high quality, it will not be able to provide students with the skills and knowledge needed to compete in the job market and contribute to economic growth.

3. Educational inequalities: Discriminations

in access to and quality of education can significantly affect the relationship between education and social and economic development. If marginalized and disadvantaged groups have less access to quality education, this can perpetuate inequality and limit their ability to participate fully in the economy.

4. Social inclusion: It is a key factor for social and economic development. Education can be a vehicle for inclusiveness, but only if the barriers that prevent certain groups in society from accessing education are addressed and provided with quality education.

5. Technology and automation: It can affect the relationship between education and social and economic development. While technology can increase the demand for specialized skills and knowledge, it can also reduce the request for jobs that can be automated. It is therefore important that education prepares students for the economy of the future and provides them with the skills needed to compete in an increasingly mechanized labor market.

A number of factors can affect the connection between social and economic development and the process of acquiring knowledge. Among these are investment in learning, quality of instruction, equalities in access, social inclusion, and the impact of technology and automation. When designing policies and programs to promote social and economic development, it is required for both governments and educational institutions to consider these factors to ensure that the process of acquiring knowledge is effective.

Education in Values and the Formation of Critical Citizens

Education in values is an increasingly relevant topic in today's world. The formation of critical citizens is fundamental to build more just and equitable societies, and values formation is a key tool to achieve this. Likewise, moral teaching refers to the process of transmitting ethical values and principles to students, with the aim of developing their character and fostering their ability to make ethical and moral decisions. This education focuses on aspects such as respect, tolerance, responsibility, honesty, solidarity, justice, and freedom.

It is suggested that students receive a social and moral education in accordance with the Basic Curriculum Design as far as it includes the formation of attitudes and values that allow them to make responsible decisions within the distinctive pluralism of contemporary society, respecting the values and beliefs of other individuals and groups. This is a project that is motivated and built on solidarity, understood as the basis on which all emotions and values are raised (González, 1990).

Education in values is directly related to the formation of critical citizens. An engaged citizen is one who has the ability to question the norms and values of their society, and to think independently and reflectively about social and political problems. Education in values fosters this critical capacity by developing in students an ethical and moral conscience that allows them to evaluate and question their social environment.

Ercilla and Tejeda (1999) understand that, although these following questions do not exhaust the themes and issues that exist, at least they introduce the analysis of values. They include questions such as: what are values, what is valuation, what relationship exists between education in values and the educational project, is it the task of the University to form values, and how can the University measure training and development? of professional values.

Some claim that new values have emerged in line with the new socio-economic and cultural paradigm. Still others argue that the problem is the existence of multivariate values, which leads to confusion and disorientation in human performance and evaluation. Perhaps, given that all this is happening, it would be worth addressing the issue. After all, man has always had to confront his own development challenges. The accelerated technological advance, globalization, and scientific progress of today's world (Ercilla & Tejeda, 1999).

One of the ways in which values education contributes to the formation of critical citizens is through the promotion of values such as tolerance and respect. These ideals encourage open-mindedness and constructive dialogue, which in turn allows students to comprehend different perspectives and points of view. By having a broader understanding of social and political reality, students can develop a deeper critical awareness.

Del Salto (2015) states that values are the cornerstone of order, balance in the personal and social sphere, and are related to the very existence of the person because they influence their behavior, shape, and configure their ideas and condition their feelings. The human being is capable of realizing, discovering, and assimilating values, and in this triple possibility is where its pedagogical meaning lies. The universal values of kindness, honesty, and respect, freedom, responsibility, equality, fraternity, solidarity, equity, and peace, complete the formation of a person in the sense of a state of peace and harmony.

In addition, education in values fosters the development of individual and collective responsibility. Values such as solidarity and social justice lead students to reflect on the importance of their role in society and their responsibility in building a more just civilization. By understanding that their individual actions have an impact on collective well-being, students can develop a deeper critical awareness and engage in finding solutions to social problems.

Another important aspect of values education is the promotion of individual freedom and autonomy. These values foster students' ability to make decisions independently and reflectively, which is vital for the development of engaged citizenship. By developing their own critical thinking ability, students can effectively question and evaluate public decisions and policies.

Concretizing, education in values is fundamental for the formation of critical citizens. This education fosters principles such as tolerance, respect, solidarity, justice, and freedom, which are essentials to develop an ethical and moral conscience that allows students to evaluate and question their social environment. The formation of critical citizens is fundamental to build more just and equitable societies, and education in values is a key tool to achieve it.

The Impact of Globalization on Education and School Culture

Before analyzing the impact of globalization on education and school culture, it is necessary to define its concept. It refers to the process of increasing interconnectedness and interdependence among countries, businesses, people, and cultures around the world. This process has accelerated in recent decades due to the liberalization of markets, the reduction of trade barriers, the improvement of information and communication technologies and the mobility of people.

Everyone should now have a position on globalization. The main achievement of the global movement opposed to globalization is to have put on the table for social and political discussion what was previously seen as the only and unquestionable path to human progress. It begins amid confusion and emotion, including mourning for the dead, typical of any great ideological debate. Therefore, the author thought it might be more useful for you, an attentive reader in your comfortable surroundings, to recall some of the facts that frame the debate rather than adding my own position to those that are published every day. Although neoliberal ideology has used it as a support for its claim to be the only possible rationality, it is an objective process and not an ideology (Castells, 2002).

Globalization is a phenomenon that has been increasing in recent decades and has had a profound impact on various aspects of human life. One of the fields that has been particularly affected by this phenomenon is that of education and school culture. In this section, we will analyze the impact of globalization in these areas and its implications for the future.

In the same vein, globalization has had a major impact on education. One of the ways in which this has manifested itself is through increased mobility of students and teachers. Nowadays, it is common for scholars to move to other countries to study and for educators to work in distinct parts of the world. This has allowed education to be more accessible and diverse.

As it was mentioned above, one of the sectors impacted by globalization is education. At all educational levels, the curious influence of the phenomenon is increasingly evident. The student, an indispensable and irreplaceable component of the educational process, it is immersed and controlled by globalization without realizing it. Many times, due to pure ignorance, the need to become aware of this phenomenon, to make it visible and to provide tools against it is ignored, actions that education must fulfill to a substantial extent (Delgado & Miguel, 2011).

Another way in which globalization has affected education is through the introduction of new teaching methods and information and communication technologies. web-based learning is an example of this. Online education has allowed students to learn from anywhere in the world and at any time, which has increased accessibility to education.

Within that same order of ideas, globalization has also had an impact on school culture. In many parts of the world, there has been a homogenization of the school system. This has manifested itself in the adoption of a common educational model worldwide, with a focus on teaching the skills and competencies needed for the global labor market. This has led to the standardization of curricula and the teaching of a number of specific skills and competences.

However, globalization has also led to greater cultural diversity in schools. This has established itself in the increase of the migrant population and linguistic diversity in classrooms. This has directed to a change in school philosophy, with a greater appreciation of cultural diversity and a greater sensitivity to the needs of students from unfamiliar social backgrounds.

The implications of globalization on education and school culture cannot be ignored. Globalization has had a major impact on education and school culture. However, this has also led to a number of implications that need to be considered. One of the main significances is the need for greater flexibility and adaptability in the education system. Globalization has led to an increased demand for online education and the need to adapt the curriculum to the needs of an increasingly connected society.

The inclusion of cultural diversity in the curriculum is also important. Students should have the opportunity to gain experience about distinct nations and traditions, as well as the challenges faced by people from different social backgrounds. This will allow them to develop greater understanding and empathy towards the experiences and perspectives of others.

In summary, the need for greater sensitivity

to cultural diversity in schools is crucial to foster understanding and respect for diverse societies. Educators must be willing to learn about distinct cultures and use that knowledge to create inclusive learning environments for all students. Positive interactions and relationships between students from unfamiliar cultural backgrounds, as well as the inclusion of way of life diversity in the curriculum, are also important in achieving this goal.

Chapter 2: The Role Of Education In Citizenship Training

This chapter focuses on the fundamental role of education in citizenship education and addresses a variety of key sub-themes. First, the relationship between school and family in the formation of students is explored, highlighting the importance of collaboration between both parts to promote effective learning. In addition, education as a social tool and its capacity to drive social change and mobility are examined.

The chapter also discusses the influence of the media on education, including the need to teach students to be critical and responsible in their consumption of information. School is presented as a means of inclusion and diversity, and the way how education can help overcome social and cultural barriers is discussed.

It also addresses the importance of education

in a country's economic development, emphasizing how quality education can improve job prospects and economic growth. The promotion of values and the culture of peace in schools are also important aspects explored in the chapter, as well as the relationship between education and the environment.

Thus, the influence of society on the education and training of students is discussed, highlighting the need for an instruction that reflects the values and requirements of the society in which it finds itself. Overall, the chapter provides a comprehensive and reflective overview of the crucial role education plays in forming responsible and active citizens in society.

The Relationship Between School and Family in the Formation of Students

The relationship between school and family is fundamental for the formation of students. Both institutions have a shared responsibility in the process of educating children and young people. It is important that they work together to ensure that students receive the support and tools necessary to succeed in their education and life in general.

The family is the first place of learning for children and is where the foundations of their education are laid. Parents and guardians have a responsibility to instill positive values, habits, and attitudes in children, all of which prepares them for the outside world. It is also important for parents to support and motivate their minors in their education, helping them set realistic goals and expectations.

On the other hand, school is the place where students learn the skills and knowledge needed to succeed in life. Teachers are tasked with delivering education and must also ensure that students receive the emotional and social support they need to grow and develop. The school should be a safe and welcoming environment for students and should be attuned to the individual needs of each one.

Regarding the nature of the bond, according to Vogels, there are four types of relationships families can have with schools and children's education: participants, clients, consumers, and partners. The suggested categories are based on the type of connection that has been made between families and education. progenies who see education as a commodity are called consumers; Families who see teachers as experts in their subjects are called clients; parents that cooperate with teachers' demands are called participating families; and parents who see education as a collaborative process that implies shared responsibility are called partners (Cárcamo, 2012 citing Colás & Contreras, 2013).

The terms "intramural" and "extramural" refer to the spatial dimensions in which family participation in the educational process develops. Intramural relates to the variety of areas that encourage parent involvement within the boundaries of the school field, or everything that happens within the school. On the other hand, the extramural refers to what happens in the home environment and supports the educational experiences of both boys and girls. In this sense, it values factors outside formal education that affect the dynamics of homeschooling. Together, intramural, and extramural cause the dynamics of the non-school field to be influenced by what happens inside the school or intramurally (Cárcamo, 2021 citing Cárcamo, 2019 & Yamamoto, 2015).

When school and family work together, they can accomplish much more than they could separately. Communication between parents and teachers is critical to making sure students are getting the education and support they need.

Parents should be involved in their children's education, through attending school meetings and events, and supporting their children in their homework and projects.

In addition, teachers can provide valuable information about students' academic progress and behavior, which can help progenitors better understand their children's needs and support them in their education. Teachers can also collaborate with parents to set realistic goals and expectations for students.

Martínez et al. (2017) argue that the values, traditions, customs, and expectations that belonged to the traditional family are inserted and formatted to accommodate new traits of family conformation and behavior. Whatever its form, however, the social, political, or personal status that encourages children to be welcomed will continue to be the ability to support, collaborate and participate in the process of realizing the goals, objectives and achievements of the children and develop skills in knowledge, expertise, and ability.

It is understood that socialization spaces that support the development of learning include both the family and the classroom. We are not sure of the functioning of each of them, which worries the educational field because, in some cases, factors such as lack of time, work commitments and obligations contracted at the time of the appointment with families, which are mere justifications, end up preventing the best possible harmony in the relationship. As a result, the school sees as part of its permanent responsibility to develop initiatives that encourage the participation of parents as active agents of the learning process, especially in situations where the academic performance of students is affected by disinterest, demotivation, and inactivity (Martínez et al., (2017).

Simply put, the relationship between school and family is crucial for the formation of students. Both institutions must work together to provide learners with the support and tools necessary to succeed in their education and in life in general. Communication, encouragement, and collaboration are essentials to establish an effective relationship between school and family.

Education as a social instrument

Education is a key social instrument that plays a vital role in the development and evolution of society. It is considered to be a crucial tool for achieving the progress and well-being of the community as a whole. Education provides people with the skills and knowledge needed to improve their lives and succeed in their work. Aran (1999) understands that, since there is no general consensus on how to define this concept or the range of interventions that fall under its scope, the term "social education" is difficult to define. However, the author provides the following definition: it is education which purpose is the development of the sociability of the person.

In addition, education can help people better understand their environment and their role in society, which in turn can improve their ability to interact with others effectively. It can also play a key role in promoting important social and ethical values, such as respect, tolerance, and equality. By teaching people about these morals, education can help build a more just and equitable society.

Education is also a means of fostering innovation and technological progress. It is needed for the development of recent technologies and the improvement of existing ones. This in turn can boost economic growth and improve the quality of life of society as a whole.

Rotger (1997) says that the noble effort made in the welfare society in support of educational practice is not always effectively accompanied by those what have been done at the postulated level, and the theoretical foundations of social education are still wobbly. Perhaps for this reason, some considerations around the idea of social education can be equally crucial to find solutions to the problems of coexistence.

As it has been stated, education is a vital public tool that has the potential to improve the lives of individuals and society.

Through learning, people can develop skills and knowledge, understand their environment, and improve their ability to interact with others. In addition, education can introduce important values and foster innovation and technological progress. Therefore, investing in education is an effective way to build a more just, equitable and prosperous society.

The Influence of the Media Communication in Education

The media has a noteworthy influence on education and the way people learn and are informed about daily day events. Today, the media include a wide variety of channels such as television, radio, newspapers, magazines, social media, and other digital instruments.

Santiago (2009) argues that the media that surround us, including cinema, television, telephone, mobile, the Internet, and the press, and others, have a significant impact on the education of our young people, often much more than we can imagine. They release a variety of messages on a daily basis that children live with without even realizing it, so they become ingrained in them.

One of the biggest benefits of media is that it can provide educational and relevant information quickly and effectively. News, educational programs, and documentaries can bring valuable information on a wide variety of topics, from science and technology to politics and culture. This can help people learn about the world around them and improve their understanding of a variety of fields.

In addition, media can also be a powerful tool for learning and teaching. Educational and documentary programs, for example, can be an effective way to introduce complex concepts in a visually appealing and easy-to-understand design. Social media and other digital formats can also be used to create learning communities and to connect students and teachers around the world.

Not only do the media have a direct impact on the education children receive, but also on the type of society that exists in and around them. In practice, we could say that society is built on the models that grow in correlation with both individual and collective types, principles developed by our politicians or leaders, large economic multinationals, minorities that share a characteristic, and others, but at the end of the day they are examples of behaviors that the media reproduce through their guidelines and rules; sometimes they serve only as a source of information, but other times they have openly consumerist or ideological backgrounds or are manifestly invented; despite this, young people accept them as true and fully incorporate them into their behaviors (Santiago, 2009).

However, it is also important to recognize that the media can have negative effects on education. For instance, inaccurate or misleading data can be disseminated through the information sources, which can confuse and mislead people. In addition, some media may promote stereotypes and prejudices that could appear harmful to certain groups of people.

The media have a major influence on education and can provide a valuable source of information and resources for learning. However, it is important to be critical of the data that are received through the media and make sure they are accurate and dependable. It is also important to use the media in a responsible and balanced manner, taking into account both the benefits and the possible negative effects on education.

The School as a Means of Inclusion and Diversity

School is an important means of inclusion and diversity, as it is a place where people from divergent backgrounds, cultures and experiences come together. By providing a safe and welcoming environment, the school can be a place where diversity is celebrated, and inclusion is encouraged.

School inclusion refers to making sure all students have equal learning opportunities and access to educational resources. This may involve providing additional support for students who need extra help, as well as tailoring the curriculum and activities to meet each student's individual needs.

Diversity in school can manifest itself in many ways, including cultural, ethnic, linguistic, and socioeconomic aspects. By including it in the classroom, students can learn about diverse cultures and viewpoints, which can help them develop a broader understanding of the world and foster respect for others.

School systems face significant structural and dynamic challenges and incapacities to meet the grand expectations placed on them in the context of the profound social, cultural, economic, and political transformations brought about by globalization and the knowledge society. An important part of them is manifested in the fact that they do not understand or advocate for fair and effective policies for the inclusion of all students in the achievement of the fundamental learnings of compulsory education. An inclusive school should, in theory, allow every student to graduate with the knowledge and credentials necessary to exercise their constitutional rights without fear of exclusion (Dominguez, 2011).

Domínguez (2011) also argues that a common curricular proposal for all basic and compulsory education is one of the fundamental requirements for inclusive education. But for the curriculum (school path) to succeed in this direction, its continuity (in the sense of its coherence and graduation) throughout all subjects, courses and stages must be ensured. All of them require students to continually adjust to changes in pedagogical culture, sometimes even within the subjects and instructors of the same course. However, it is during this shift from primary to secondary education that the most at-risk students face the greatest threat of being expelled from the regular education system.

The issue is a pending task to improve, and all actors are called to play their role in the conquest of inclusion and diversity. It must be recognized that efforts are being made to address the non-observance of such actions. The purpose of addressing this issue has been to raise awareness among citizens in general about having a more inclusive society that attends to plurality.

If anything, school can also be a place where issues related to diversity and inclusion, such as racism, discrimination, and bullying, are addressed. By providing a safe space for students to talk about these issues, the school can help raise awareness and foster inclusion and acceptance. By celebrating diversity and providing support to learners in need, the school can help create an environment where all of them feel valued and respected.

The Importance of Education in the Economic Development of a Country

Education is a basic tool in the economic development of a country. It provides citizens with the skills and knowledge needed to participate in the economy, whether as employees, entrepreneurs, or businesspeople. Here are some of the ways education influences economic development:

1. Fostering innovation: Education promotes innovation by equipping individuals with the abilities and understanding needed for generating creative and inventive concepts and answers. Consequently, this could result in the emergence of fresh goods, technologies, and services, which have the potential to fuel economic progress.

2. Increased productivity: Education can also develop worker production. People with higher levels of instruction tend to have more advanced skills and are better prepared to face the challenges of the labor market. This can lead to greater efficiency in production processes and an improvement in the quality of the work done.

3. Improving employability: Education can improve people's workforce readiness,

which can lead to higher labor force participation and therefore an increase in production and consumption. Workers with higher levels of education tend to have more employment options and greater opportunities for advancement.

4. Fostering entrepreneurship: Education can foster Self-employment by providing people with the skills and knowledge needed to start and run their own businesses. This can lead to the growth of new companies and increased competition in the market, which in turn can stimulate the economy.

Many researchers in the field have disagreed about the importance of human capital as a factor of economic development in nations. In industrialized nations, the effects of education on progress can be roughly estimated. It is critical to emphasize that developed countries have significantly more economic literature on the demand for education than developing countries, largely as a result of theoretical and empirical advances made in the United States of America and Europe (Cavero et at., 2023).

At its core, education is fundamental

to a country's economic development. It can foment innovation, increase productivity, improve employability, and foster entrepreneurship, which can lead to an increase in production and consumption, and sustainable economic growth.

The Relationship Between Education and the Environment

The relationship between education and the environment is fundamental to achieving sustainable development in today's world. Ecological education refers to a continuous learning process that aims to increase awareness of climate-related issues and encourage responsible action to preserve and protect the Ecosystem.

Here are some ways in which environmental education can influence the habitat:

1. Awareness and understanding: Ecocultural education can help people understand how their individual actions can affect the ecosystem. Through knowledge, schooling can raise awareness about the importance of preserving and protecting the environment.

2. Behavior change: Earth-friendly education can also encourage lifestyle adjustment. By understanding how their actions can impact the ambience, people can make more informed and responsible lifestyle choices, such as reducing their carbon

footprint, recycling, and using sustainable transport.

3. Policies and actions: Environmental education can also lead to the formulation of strategies to care the planet. As more people become aware of environmental issues, they can pressure governments and businesses to implement more sustainable programs.

4. Innovation and entrepreneurship: Environmental education can stimulate innovation and sustainable business acumen, as people who understand ecological issues can identify fresh solutions and business opportunities.

If the ability to highlight and integrate the best qualities of those who make up a community is the basis of society life, then education must give adequate answers to the problems it encounters as a tool for socialization and development of a critical mentality. One of them, possibly the most important at a time of global change such as the one we are currently experiencing, is to reorient our way of life towards austerity, moderation, and simplicity to break the vicious circle of economic accumulation for a select few at the expense of the poverty of the majority of people and the destruction of the environment (Novo, (2009).

Novo (2009) understands that there are at least two insurmountable challenges facing education: the ecological challenge, which involves helping to educate and train not only children and young people, but also managers, planners, and decision-makers, to help them orient their values and behaviors towards a harmonious relationship with nature. The social challenge, which in a society where wealth is unequally distributed, forces us to make radical changes.

In short, environmental education is fundamental for the sustainable development of the planet. By fostering awareness, behavior change, policies and actions, innovation and entrepreneurship, eco-literacy can help preserve and protect the habitat for present and future generations.

The Influence of Society on the Formation of Students

Society is a key factor in the formation of students since it is the environment in which they develop and learn to interact with the world around them. Learners are influenced by a variety of social factors, such as family, culture, media, and the community in which they live.

The family is the first social environment in which students develop. Parents and other household members are the primary role models for them, and can influence the way they think, act, and perceive the world. Education and values passed down at home can significantly affect how scholars relate to others, make decisions, and see themselves.

Culture is another important social factor that influences the training of students. Society can influence their way of seeing the world, values and beliefs, perception of right and wrong, and their sense of identity. Culture can also influence how learners communicate and relate to others, and how they perceive and process information.

Martínez (2006) understands that the university is the stage where the body of knowledge is acquired that will allow the future graduate to start in the exercise of a profession successfully and advance in the understanding of a field of knowledge, so that students can, if they wish, dedicate themselves to research, specialization and go deep into their development field of study. However, it is less clear that one specifically learns a set of ethical and civic knowledge at a university; certainly, it is not for everyone.

In today's socio-cultural environment, universities are suitable places to learn about professional and cultural topics in their broadest sense, as well as about human ethical and moral nature. In our opinion, it would be a mistake not to make use of this function since it is the responsibility of any educational institution to advance the pedagogical strength of the university in relation to learning and training linked to the ethical and moral dimensions of students (Martinez, 2006).

Another point to consider is the following: Sánchez (2009) understands that information and communication technologies (ICT), which have gained prominence in today's society, based on information and knowledge, have an increasing impact on education. In this scenario, new educational paradigms emerge, including blended learning (combined) and e-learning, also known as Internet-based learning. These new strategies can help in the process of adaptation to the new European Higher Education Area (EHEA) and, in general, in the process of renewal and improvement of academic institutions, specifically in higher education.

The media also have an enormous influence on the training of students. Television, social media, and other tools can affect the way students see the world, their knowledge and perception of current events, as well as their values and attitudes.

Learners can be influenced by the messages conveyed in the media and may adopt opinions or behaviors that are reflected in what they see and hear.

Finally, the society in which students live can influence their training. A community's social relationships, infrastructure, services, and culture can affect how students relate to others, their sense of association and belonging, and their worldview.

In conclusion, society has a considerable influence on the formation of students. Family, culture, media, and community are key factors that can affect how they think, act, and relate to the world around them. Therefore, it is important that educators, parents, and other members of the society take steps to foster a positive and healthy social environment that promotes the well-rounded upbringing of students.

Chapter 3: The Influence Of Culture On The Educational System

Culture is a principal factor in the formation of a country's education system. The way a society values knowledge and education can have a significant impact on the way it is structured and taught in the pedagogy system. In Chapter 3, the influence of culture on the schooling system will be explored through analyzing how a society's beliefs, values, and traditions can affect the educational process. The relationship between culture and education in different countries and regions of the world will be examined, as well as how it can influence the selection of educational content, teaching methodology and the assessment of student achievement. In addition, current trends in way of life and education will be analyzed, and the opportunities and challenges facing the education system in the current society context will be identified. Ultimately, this chapter will deepen the understanding of how culture influences the education system, and how this can affect students and society at large.

Relationship Between Culture and Education: Concepts and Definitions

The relationship between culture and education is complex and multifaceted and can be defined in several ways. Warnier (2001) suggests that the term "globalization of customs" refers to the global exchange of cultural goods that generates strong opinions. Some link it to the promise of a democratic planet united by a universal culture, the world which size has been reduced to that of a global village by the media.

Here are some key concepts and definitions related to this topic:

- **Culture**: It refers to the set of knowledge, values, traditions, beliefs, customs, and behaviors shared by a group of people. It can be expressed through music, art, literature, religion, technology, politics, and other aspects of social life. Echeverria (2019) argues that the cultural aspect of social existence is not only always present as a factor influencing individual and group behavior in the social world but can also make a significant contribution to the course of history.

- **Education**: It refers to the teaching and learning process that aims to develop students' knowledge, skills, attitudes, and values. Education can be formal (in a school or university), non-formal (in a workshop or course) or informal (through everyday experience). In addition, education can be non-presence, which according to García (1987), citing Armengol (1982), distance learning encompasses a wide range of different forms and pedagogical approaches that share the characteristic that teachers and students do not physically fulfill by meeting regularly in places designated for educational purposes.
- **Socialization**: It refers to the process by which individuals learn and acquire the norms, values, and behaviors of their culture and society. Socialization can occur through family, friends, school, media, and other social (public) institutions. According to Lozano (1988) "socialization is the process of learning in accordance with the norms, habits and customs of the group. It is the ability to conduct oneself in accordance with social expectations" (p.8).
- **Multiculturalism**: it refers to the coexistence of multiple cultures and the promotion of cultural diversity in a society, where "culture" refers to racial, religious, or ethnic groups as shown by traditional behaviors, customs presumptions, and values, thought patterns, and methods of communication. By exposing students to diverse cultural perspectives and experiences, multiculturalism can be

seen as a way to improve education. Multicultural library services encompass both the distribution of multiethnic information to all types of library users and the provision of its services that are especially targeted at historically underserved groups (Chu et al, 2005).

Intersectionality: It refers to the way a person's multiple identities and experiences (such as gender, race, social class, sexual orientation, and disability) interact and intersect to affect their position in society. Interconnectedness can be relevant in education by addressing how unfamiliar cultural groups may have different educational experiences.

Simply put, intersectionality is the awareness of mutually reinforcing relationships between various structural sources of inequality, also known as "social organizers." It is a method that emphasizes how the social categories mentioned before are constructed and relate to each other, in both "natural" and "biological" way (Méndez, 2014).

In short, culture and education are closely

related, and can influence each other. the former can affect the way culture is taught and learned in the education system, and the latter can affect how culture is transmitted and valued. Understanding the relationship between these two categories is required for effective and equitable education in an increasingly diverse world.

Culture as a Framework for Teaching and Learning

Culture can be seen as an important frame of reference for teaching and learning in the education system. It influences the way learners perceive the world, build their knowledge, and relate to others, so it is needed that educators consider their students' culture when planning and conducting their teaching.

First, culture can influence the selection of educational content. It can determine which topics and skills are most valued and relevant to a particular society. Educators should take into account the cultural norms, practices, and values of their students when selecting educational content to ensure that it is relevant and meaningful to them.

Second, society can also influence the teaching methodology used in the classroom. Teaching strategies and pedagogical approach should take into account students' code of conduct differences and be tailored to meet students' individual needs. For example, some students may prefer to learn through participation and group work, while others may be more comfortable with more traditional, teacher-centered approach.

Third, culture can influence how student achievement is assessed. Standards and evaluation criteria must be traditionally relevant and fair to all learners. For example, some students may be more accustomed to a memory-based assessment style, while others may be more accustomed to a more practical evaluation method.

The importance of culture in the teaching of a second language has been reassessed since the advent of the communicative method occurred. Learning a language also involves becoming familiar with a set of rules of use the moment it becomes clear that mastering a language involves more than just learning a particular linguistic system. It also involves developing the ability to use it in communication. Interlocutors give meaning to words when they relate them to the context of conversational situation in which they find themselves and to their prior knowledge of the outside world (Gómez et al., citing Ruiz, 2000).

In conclusion, culture can be seen as an essential frame of reference for teaching and learning in the education system. By considering students' code of conduct differences, educators can help create a more inclusive and meaningful learning environment for all students. In doing so, educators can help foster cross-cultural understanding and acceptance, and prepare students for an increasingly globalized and diverse world.

The importance of Interculturality in Education

Interculturality in education refers to the appreciation and promotion of cultural diversity in the classroom and in the education system in general. It is important to recognize the cultural diversity of students and use it as a resource in the teaching and learning process. Interculturality in education promotes cosmopolitan understanding, acceptance, and respect towards distinct cultures, which can have a positive impact on society.

First, interculturality in education can help students develop diverse skills. By being exposed to diverse cultures and perspectives, the students are given the opportunity to understand and appreciate cultural differences and develop skills to interact with people from unfamiliar social backgrounds. This can help foster empathy, effective communication, and collaboration in an increasingly diverse world.

Secondly, interculturality in education can

contribute to social inclusion. It can help reduce discrimination and social exclusion by promoting respect for and acceptance of all customs. This can foster a sense of belonging and community among students from distinct cultural backgrounds and help create a more inclusive and equitable society.

Thirdly, interculturality in education can be a tool to preserve and promote cultural diversity. Cross-cultural school can help students understand and appreciate diverse cultures and traditions, which can help preserve and promote social convention in an increasingly connected world.

Rehaag (2010) understands that, since we live in a globalized world with societies that are changing very rapidly, the school has the responsibility to promote a vision towards respect for diversity. The task of educating in the context of these experiences lies in the teaching of intercultural competences. The encounter with cultural diversity is becoming an increasingly common occurrence in everyday life.

Schmelkes (2004) argues that communication technologies offer us the opportunity to have a more virtual contact with other cultures and, inevitably, an epistemological reflection that, consciously or unconsciously, makes us relativize our own culture. Our society can no longer be understood as culture when it is faced with the daily contact with diversity. It is undeniable that the process has been lengthy and uneven. The impression that globalization forces a model of production, consumption, coexistence, entertainment, and conception of the world cannot be denied.

In conclusion, interculturality in education is important to foster global understanding, social inclusion, and the preservation of cultural diversity. By valuing and promoting pluralism in the classroom, students can be helped to develop intercultural skills and foster a sense of community and acceptance towards all cultures. Inclusive education can be a powerful tool to build a more inclusive, just, and equitable society.

The Role of Culture in the Formation of Values and Attitudes in Education

Culture plays a fundamental role in the formation of values and attitudes in education, since it is through it that the norms, beliefs, and values that govern the behavior of people in a society are transmitted and internalized. In education, culture becomes a frame of reference for the formation of principles in students.

First, society provides the context in which students' moral, and ethic develop. Every culture has its own values and norms that are passed down through generations and that influence the way people see the world and relate to others. In the classroom, teachers can use culture to provide meaningful context for learning, which can help students understand how their own attitudes and values are influenced by their customs.

Secondly, culture can be used as a tool for the formation of values and attitudes. Culture can transmit values and norms that are considered important in a society, such as respect, tolerance, honesty, and responsibility. Teachers can use culture to teach these Ideals and principles, and help students internalize and apply them in their daily lives.

Third, culture can be used to foster diversity and inclusion. By recognizing and valuing tradition and Inclusivity, teachers can help students develop attitudes and values that foster inclusion and respect for all cultures and perspectives. This can help create a more inclusive and nurturing learning environment for all students.

Molina (2012) understands that one of the principles of education is the formation of values because one of its objectives is to influence how the student's personality develops integrally. Its principles and methods of application can be found in a variety of disciplines, including sociology, psychology, education, and philosophy. The author further explains that his lectures and classes generally focus on fostering knowledge, skills, competencies, and habits in a particular science because teaching values can sometimes be a cover for university professors who lack psych pedagogical knowledge.

In short, culture plays a vital role in the formation of values and attitudes in education. By providing a context for learning, transmitting morals and norms, and fostering diversity and inclusion, culture can be used as a powerful tool to help students develop ideals and principles that enable them to be responsible and engaged citizens in an increasingly diverse and globalized society.

The Challenges of Intercultural Education

Intercultural education is an educational modality that seeks to promote respect, appreciation and understanding of the unfamiliar cultures present in a society. Although this type of learning can be very enriching and beneficial for students, it also presents certain challenges that must be addressed for it to be effective. Below, there are some of the main obstacles of intercultural education:

1. Teacher training: For intercultural education to be effective, it is necessary to have well-trained educators in this educational modality. They should be qualified to work with students from distinct cultures and be able to tailor their teaching to the needs of each cultural group.
2. Access to resources and materials: Intercultural education requires educational materials and resources that reflect cultural diversity. it is needed that they be developed in such a way so that they enable teachers to teach about diverse cultures in an accurate and respectful manner.

3. Acceptance of cultural diversity: One of the biggest challenges of intercultural education is to foster cultural tolerance among students. It is necessary that students learn to value and respect the cultural differences of their peers and to understand that these differences enrich society.

4. The inclusion of all students: In intercultural education it is important to ensure that all students feel included and represented in the classroom. It is necessary that the distinct cultures present in the classroom are respected and all the participants are encouraged.

5. Overcoming prejudices and stereotypes: Intercultural education seeks to break with them. It is necessary to foster respect and understanding of the different cultures present in society so that students can overcome the prejudices and stereotypes they may have.

Aguirre et al. (2015) understand that, in view of the fact that their nation (Ecuador), which identifies itself as "intercultural" and "plurinational", is actually home to numerous ethnic communities and Indigenous nationalities, as well as Afro-Ecuadorian, Montubia and immigrant communities, it is necessary to ask: Is it possible to live interculturality in the Ecuadorian educational context? In other words, is something what is known as interculturality and which implies numerous demands, applicable in the national reality in Ecuador. As it can be seen, these conditions represent a challenge for educators.

A new task in the current education system is pedagogical innovations in intercultural teaching, so teachers are addressing this problem in order to prepare students for the realities of the outside world. Thus, to adapt the learning environment to the needs of the students of this new generation, the teachers must update their knowledge. (Berrenzuela et al., 2021).

To recap, intercultural education is a modality of learning that presents certain challenges and that must be addressed to be effective. Teacher training, access to adequate resources and materials, acceptance of cultural diversity, inclusion of all students and overcoming prejudices and stereotypes are some of the challenges facing intercultural education. By addressing these struggles, it can be ensured that intercultural learning is an effective tool for fostering respect, appreciation and understanding of the distinct cultures present in a society.

The Influence of Cultural Beliefs and Practices on Education and its Relationship to Religious Education

Culture is a set of values, beliefs, practices, and customs that characterize a particular society. These elements can influence education in a variety of ways, from the strategy subjects are taught to the path educational institutions are organized. In addition, in some cases, cultural beliefs and practices may be directly related to religious education.

Ibáñez et al. (2006) state that, since the Universal Declaration of Human Rights, religious freedom has emerged as a way to foster the identities of various social groups. In an open society, the freedom to teach religion in schools has arisen naturally, in accordance with the constitutional traditions of the various nations. The teaching of the Catholic religion in schools, in particular, is entirely consistent with the history of Christianity, which has always held that God is the Truth.

However, the presence of a distinct religious education curriculum in schools does not imply that there is a single optimal approach to teaching it or that it must necessarily be incorporated as such. The decision to include religious education in the curriculum, as well as the manner in which it is merged, will primarily rely on the constitutional standards of each country. It is evident that the matter of religious education will not be resolved uniformly in nations with confessional states, those within the European Union that prioritize secularism, or those seeking to acknowledge the religious beliefs prevalent within their population (Ibáñez et al., 2006).

Religious education is an educational modality that seeks to transmit the values and beliefs of a certain religion to students. In many societies, religion is an important part of association and therefore this type of education can be a way of transmitting cultural values and beliefs through it.

Cultural beliefs and practices can impact education in a number of ways. For example, cultural beliefs about the importance of education can influence how parents and students value learning and the importance they place on it in their lives. Cultural beliefs about learning can also affect the way subjects are taught and the methodology is used in educational institutions.

In the case of religious education, social beliefs and practices related to it can influence the way values and beliefs are taught. For example, in some cultures, religion is especially important and is taught from an early age in theology (specialized) schools. In other ones, religion is seen as a personal matter and is taught less formally.

Rueda et al. (2019) understand that the disciplinary nature of school religious education (RSE) requires considering its object of study as a fundamental component of the epistemological statute. From our point of view, the religious fact such as: phenomenon, experience, and dimension can be studied by the RSE. To determine their purpose, content, and didactics, it is necessary to first evaluate the contribution of the disciplines that support them (religious studies and phenomenology, spiritual and interreligious theology, religious psychology, among others). None of these can be challenged. Objects of study contain an enormous wealth because, although they approach religion from a particular approach and put their accent already on its objectification or its subjectivation, they know that the religious is something proper to the human.

However, it is important to note that cultural beliefs and practices are not immutable and can change over time. For example, in some countries, religious education has lost importance due to the secularization of society and the growing separation between religion and the State. In other cases, cultural beliefs and practices may conflict with formal instruction and may hinder access to education for some social groups.

Thus, cultural beliefs and practices can have an enormous influence on learning and, in some cases, may be related to religious. It is important to recognize the importance of these cultural influences in education and work to ensure that teaching is accessible and relevant to all students, regardless of their cultural and religious beliefs. In addition, it is important to keep in mind that cultural beliefs and practices are not immutable and can change over time, so it is vital to be attentive to these transformations and adapt to them to offer a more appropriate and effective education.

Chapter 4: The Role Of The Media In The Formation Of Public Opinion

The role of the media in shaping public opinion on education is a topic of great relevance today. It has a significant impact on public perception of education and its different sub-themes. From the influence of the media on the education agenda to its relationship with digital learning and the development of technological skills, the media plays a key role in shaping public opinion about pedagogy.

This chapter will explore some of the key issues related to the influence of the media on public perception of education. The relationship between the media and the educational agenda will be analyzed through examining its impact on public policies in this area. The connection of the media with digital education and its influent on the development of technological skills will also be studied.

In addition, the importance of specialized journalism in the coverage of educational issues and its role in citizenship education will be addressed. The challenges of education in the twenty-first century under the influence of the media and public opinion will also be explored. This chapter will also provide an overview of the influence of the media on shaping public opinion on education and its sub-themes and analyze the role of the media in citizenship education and political decision-making.

Influence of the Media on Public Perception of Education

The media have a notable influence on molding public perception of education. The way they portray educational information holds considerable sway over how individuals perceive the education system and its associated matters. The media's impact on public understanding of education predominantly stems from its capacity to selectively emphasize specific aspects of the reality of learning and transmit them across various channels and mediums.

According to Marino (2005), the media and digital information technologies create a parallel informal education system with its own codes, languages, norms, and values. Similar to what happens in a regular school, the effects of this parallel institution act both immediately and over time. This occurs because of the fact that both children and adults spend the same amount of time online and interact with media.

One of the ways the media influence public perception of education is through topic selection and news making. It can highlight certain problems or aspects of the education system, such as the quality of teaching, access to education, violence in schools, and other ones. In doing so, the media can create a perception that certain issues are more important than others, which can influence public opinion and political decision-making.

Through the media, citizens can find out about events in their city, nation, or the entire world. The idea that there was a time before radio, television or newspapers is surprising. Since they serve crucial functions in the daily lives of citizens and in the way they interact with the political system, it is now impossible for many people to imagine a world without any of these forms of communication. We can instantly access what is happening anywhere on the planet, quickly gather information from various sources, mobilize for a compelling cause, and defend the social and political rights of someone who is far away thanks to them. We also know what rulers do (or do not do), what they are doing and what they are not doing. Despite the media's propensity to claim ownership of the public's voice and impersonate its representatives, in reality, the media are not elected or controlled by the people they purport to represent (Freidenberg, 2004).

Furthermore, the media can shape public perception of education by carefully choosing sources and featuring the opinions of experts they interview. By selectively picking sources that align with specific viewpoints or opinions on education, the media can potentially present a skewed picture of the true educational landscape. Additionally, when education experts are portrayed as unquestionable authorities, their opinions may be perceived as absolute truths, which further impacts public perception.

In that same vein, Ramonet (2013)

understands that the media are a problem for democracies because they do not serve the interests of the public and, instead, serve those of the corporations that own them. In addition, due to the general conditions of the structure of journalism today, such as the advent of the Internet and the general acceleration of information, the media are now less reliable. In any case, we observe a conflict between society and mass communication in most democratic nations.

Another important aspect is the way in which the media cover educational issues. Often, the news focuses on negative aspects of pedagogy, such as poor academic performance, lack of resources or violence in schools, which can create a negative perception of teaching in public opinion. In addition, the media can present a stereotypical image of students, teachers, and education staff, which can influence public insight of these actors in the academic system.

Thus, the effect of the media on public

perception of education is significant. It can impact public opinion through the selection of topics, sources, and the way they cover educational issues. It is important that the media present a balanced and accurate picture of the education system, which can contribute to more informed decision-making based on pedagogical reality.

The Relationship Between the Media and the Education Agenda and its Impact on Public Policy

The relationship between the media and the education agenda is close and complex. News can influence the academic plan, that is, the issues and problems that are discussed in the public and political sphere in relation to education. In turn, curriculum can have an impact on public policies, that is, on the decisions and actions taken by governments in relation to school. In this sense, the media can have a significant impact on public policies on education.

The relationship between the media and the learning objectives is largely due to the ability of reporters to select and highlight certain educational issues. News industry can choose certain topics to focus on, such as the quality of teaching, access to education, violence in schools, among others, and can produce news and reports that generate interest and attention in public opinion. In doing so, the media can influence the educational agenda, issues that are discussed and debated in the public and political sphere.

In addition, the media can have an impact on the way educational issues are discussed and addressed on the public agenda. The media may select sources and experts who support certain opinions or views on education, which may influence the way the issue is approached and discussed in the public and political sphere. They can also present education experts as undisputed authorities, which can cause the opinions of these experts to be seen as the absolute truth.

It is impossible to analyze teacher training and employment policies outside the productive environments that teachers use daily for the performance of their duties. From this point of view, it is possible to observe the distance between on the agenda´s topics, which are discussed at the global and regional levels and supported by international and regional organizations, working groups supported by these agencies and ministerial technicians, and the objective and subjective conditions of educators and educational practices in the context of each of the countries of the Region (Feldfeber, 2007).

As for the impact of the media on public policies in education, they can have a significant effect. The media can influence collective opinion and political decision-making by highlighting certain educational issues on the public agenda. The media can also inform and educate the public on certain educational issues, which can generate a demand for action from governments.

The strategic importance of the management of the mass media is clear from the very definition of "information siege", which explains the narrative, ideological and economic closure of hegemony in media terms. In situations where information cannot be manipulated, such control is exercised in numerous ways, from organizational policies given as owners of multimedia conglomerates to the use of force in the service of the same interests (Sel, 2009).

However, it is important to note that the influence of the media on public policies in education is complex and depends on multiple factors, such as the political system, and culture, the capacity of pedagogical institutions and citizen participation. In addition, the media are not the only actors influencing public policies on education, as there are also other participants, such as governments, interest groups and civil society.

Science, with all its derivatives and alternatives, is an essential component of modern societies, but sometimes it seems that thousands of technological and scientific artifacts, derived from research, are already in use without thinking about how or why. This forces communities to follow the dictates of the market of this type of elements, which is even worse than living unprepared of the numerous opportunities that STI (Science,

Technology, and Innovation) offers them to improve their existence, develop their potential and have a journey through the world more promising, with more comforts, but also leaving greater legacies or traces (Zuluaga, 2017).

In short, the relationship between the media and the education agenda is close and complex, and news can have a significant impact on public policies in school programs. It is important that the media present a balanced and accurate picture of the education system, which can contribute to more informed decision-making based on educational reality.

Relationship of Media and Digital Education and its Impact on the Development of Technological Skills

The relationship between media and digital education is increasingly relevant due to the growing importance of technologies in people's daily and working lives. The media can have a significant impact on the development of computer-based skills, both through the provision of educational content and programs related to technologies, and through the way in which digital education is delivered and discussed.

First, the media can offer educational content and programs related to technologies, which can contribute to the development of digital skills in people. For example, media outlets may offer online education programs, tutorials, or educational apps that teach people how to use different technologies, such as programming, graphic design, data analysis, and others. These contents can be particularly useful for people who want to improve their technological skills and be enhanced in the digital world.

In addition, the media can be a source of inspiration for people who want to develop cyber skills. For example, through the coverage of success stories in the technological field, the media can motivate people to acquire information technology-related skills and knowledge to develop their own projects and ventures.

Amar et al. (2010) express that the media have altered daily life and changed the habits and behaviors of the population. A growing value is how interconnected the world is. In the same way that media allow us to dream keeping our eyes open, bringing us closer to realities and leading us to imagine situations, mediatized society lets us communicate through devices and generate discourses that impact the population. However, the most important aspect of this is that things can still get better (for tech pessimists, the worst is yet to come). What we have seen simply serves as a reminder of how much there is to learn and how varied the field of learning are.

On the other hand, the media can also have an impact on the way digital education is served and discussed. The media can be a source of information about the latest trends and technological advances in the educational field, which can help people keep up with new teaching tools and methods in the digital world. In addition, the media can be a space for debate and discussion on the challenges and opportunities posed by virtual learning, which can help society reflect on the role of technology in education and in culture in general.

However, it is important to note that the relationship between media and digital education can also have some challenges. Sometimes, the media can contribute to the creation of stereotypes about certain technological skills, such as programming or engineering, which can discourage certain groups of people from acquiring technological skills. In addition, the media can contribute to the creation of a digital divide, as not all people have access to the same technologies and resources to acquire technological skills.

In conclusion, the relationship between media and digital education can have a significant impact on the development of technological skills in people. The media can be a source of inspiration, information and education for those people who want to improve their computer skills. However, it is important to take into account the challenges that this relationship can present, and work to reduce the digital divide and promote a balanced and accurate picture of technological skills in society.

Importance of Specialized Journalism in Covering Educational Issues and its Role in Citizenship Education

Journalism that specializes in covering school issues plays a vital role in promoting civic awareness. By providing accurate and relevant information about the educational landscape, it fosters public discourse and critical examination of the challenges and opportunities within the broader societal framework. The significance of this specialized journalism lies in its contribution to citizen engagement and informed participation.

To begin with, specialized journalism focused on matters related to schools and learning holds significance due to its ability to keep society well-informed about the progress and obstacles within the realm of schooling. By means of news coverage, reports, and interviews with experts in the field, media outlets have the capacity to circulate pertinent and current details regarding policies, programs, and initiatives being conducted nationwide. This becomes particularly crucial in a context where education is widely recognized as a fundamental driver of both social and economic advancement.

Furthermore, specialized journalism focusing on matters pertaining to schools and learning holds the potential to foster discussions and introspection concerning the obstacles and prospects presented by the system of instruction. By seeking the viewpoints and analysis of experts in the field, media outlets can present diverse perspectives on significant topics related to schools, encompassing aspects like inclusivity, educational excellence, technological integration, and more. Such coverage aids society in gaining a deeper comprehension of the hurdles faced by the educational system and prompts reflection on ways to enhance the state of education within the nation.

According to Cerna (2019), what is known as

news is created through the processing of reality and the continuous flow of news interpreted by the journalist. Although few authors have taken the risk of defining the news in this way, it is possible to argue conceptually that it can only be the original. As we have already seen, this argument responds to the fact that the news has in its conception a principle of novelty, scoop, and originality (some without being exclusive of the others). It is important to bear in mind that the revelation of an event as news also supposes a response to the present as a dependent binomial.

On a different note, another important aspect of journalism specialized in educational issues is its ability to make visible the voices and experiences of key actors in the education system, such as teachers, students, and parents. Through the coverage of stories and testimonies of these participants, the media can make the classrooms and the educational system's realities known. This can help to sensitize society about the needs and demands of these actors, as well as to make visible the good practices and successful experiences that can be replicated in other contexts.

Finally, journalism specialized in educational issues can also contribute to the formation of a critical and education-informed citizen. By providing relevant and up-to-date information about the teaching system, the media can help society better understand educational processes and make better decisions about children's education and upbringing. In addition, by promoting debate and reflection on educational issues, the media can encourage citizen participation in decision-making about the school system and in promoting quality knowledge for all.

In conclusion, journalism specialized in the coverage of learning challenges has a crucial role in citizen education, since it is responsible for informing, analyzing, and reflecting on relevant educational matters. Likewise, it promotes dialogue and national participation, and contributes to transparency and accountability in the education system. Therefore, it is required to have journalists specialized in this sphere who can provide rigorous and verified information and contribute to critical and informed members of the community.

The Challenges of Education in the XXI Century Faced with the Influence of the Media and Public Opinion

In the twenty-first century, education confronts a number of challenges in terms of the influence of the media and public opinion. Nowadays, the media play an increasingly vital role in shaping social consensus about education, which can have a significant impact on curriculum´s policies and practices.

Beresaluce (2008) indicates that numerous incidents throughout history have had a significant effect on the functioning of schools today. Similarly, the ideas of eminent teachers broaden and enrich the curriculum through fostering renewal movements that open exceptional schools which serve as role models. However, in the field of current social values, which are transmitted through informal education, today's society uses violence as an accepted, sacralized behavior, which is not only recognized and valued socially, but is also used as a means of entertainment for children and young people in their spare time.

The following are some of the main challenges facing education in the twenty-first century under the influence of the media and public opinion:

1. Disinformation and fake news: These are a big problem at the moment and can have a negative impact on society perception of education. The media can spread misinformation or prejudiced news about school, which can influence public opinion and education policies. It is therefore critical to foster media literacy and society's aggressive capacity to identify and evaluate the information they receive.

2. The digital split: The influence of the media can also accentuate the digital gap in education. Lack of access to information and communication technologies can prevent students from having access to the information and knowledge they need to succeed in education. The media can also focus on advanced and novel technologies, which can cause access problems and lack of instructions in many schools.

3. The need for digital education: It has become increasingly important in the twenty-first century, and the media can play a significant role in promoting virtual learning and developing technological skills. However, it is also important to ensure that digital education is equitable and accessible to all, regardless of socio-economic or geographical background.

4. The relationship between the media and the education agenda: The media can influence the learning objectives and public policies, which can have a significant impact on education. It is important for the media to focus on reporting objectively and critically on school issues, rather than pushing political or ideological agendas.

5. The need for critical civic education: In a world where the media have an increasingly key role in shaping public opinion about education, it is needed to encourage social justice. Critical citizenship education involves the development of skills to evaluate and question the received information, which can contribute to an informed citizenry committed to improving education.

In short, journalism specialized in the coverage of educational issues is indispensable to inform society about issues that affect school in all its dimensions. In addition, targeted reporting in education has a vital role in the formation of conscious and committed citizens and in improving the quality of teaching. It is therefore necessary for the media to give priority to covering pedagogical issues and for the training of journalists specializing in education to be encouraged.

Conclusions

The book "School and Society: Who is Shaping Whom?" shows that education and society are intrinsically related and concludes that education is a continuous process that adapts to social and cultural changes. In addition, the importance of finding a balance between tradition and innovation in education must be considered to ensure its relevance and effectiveness in today's world.

Through these four chapters, a broad reflection on the interrelation between education and society is presented, which is an indicator of the evolution of the school and the need to adapt educational practices to social and cultural changes and consider them as a priority in the training of our students. The role of education in citizen education and the challenges and opportunities presented in this regard are highlighted. Likewise, the influence of culture in the educational system and the need to recognize and respect cultural diversity in the classroom are pending social issues that the school must implement and promote. No less important has been the knowledge of the role of the media in shaping public opinion on education.

In short, the book "School and Society: Who is Shaping Whom?" invites us to reflect on the importance of adapting education to social and cultural changes, to ensure its relevance and effectiveness in the formation of critical citizens committed to society. It is a fundamental work for all those interested in the field of education and sociology, and those who wish to deepen the understanding of interrelationship between education and society. It is noted that school and society shape each other continuously. This has been the most relevant conclusion provided by the consulted literature.

References

Aguerrondo, I. (2017). The new paradigm of education for the XXI century.

Aguilar Piñal, F. (1988). Between school and university: secondary education in the eighteenth century. *Journal of Education.*

Aguirre, É. F. H., & Mantuano, N. C. (2015). Interculturality as a challenge for Ecuadorian education. *Sophia, Collection of Philosophy of Education,* (18), 147-162.

Amar Rodriguez, V. M. (2010). Education in digital media. *Pixel-Bit.*

Aran, A. P. (1999). *Didactics in Social Education: Teaching and Learning Outside School* (Vol. 135). Graó.

Beresaluce Díez, R. (2008). Quality as a challenge in early childhood education schools at the beginning of the XXI century: the schools of Reggio Emilia, by Loris Malaguzzi, as a model to follow in educational practice.

Berrezueta, S. M. S., Gallegos, K. H. G., & Lazo, E. S. (2021). Pedagogical innovations in intercultural education: A challenge for teaching practice. *Electronic Journal Academic Interview (REEA)*, *2*(8), 121-141.

Cárcamo, H., & Jarpa-Arriagada, C. (2021). Weakness in the family-school relationship, evidence from the perspective of future teachers. *Educational Perspective*, *60*(1), 58-80.

Castells, M. (2002). Globalization and anti-globalization. *JE Stiglitz and M. Barlow, Panic in Globalization. Bogotá, Colombia: Fica.*

Cavero Fromme, S., Esteban García, J., Girón Espinoza, A., Ríos Tuesta, F., & Vicente Chaparro, A. (2023). Relationship between education and economic development.

Chu, C. M., Nikonorova, E., & Pyper, J. (2005). Defining "Multiculturalism".

Davini, M. C. (1996). Conflicts in the evolution of didactics. *The demarcation of general didactics and special didactics (chapter 2). Camilloni, Alice,*

41-73.

Davini, M. C. (2008). Teaching methods. *General didactics for teachers and professors. Buenos Aires: Santillana.*

De la Torre Gómez, A. F. (2003). The Socratic method and the van Hidele model. *Math Readings, 24*(2), 99-121.

De Zubiría Samper, J. (2019). The challenges to education in the XXI century.

Del Salto Bello, M. W. A. (2015). Education in values: proposal of a strategy. *Medisan,* 19(11), 1421-1429.

Delgado, P. S., & Miguel, J. C. R. (2011). Globalization and education: repercussions of the phenomenon on students and alternatives to it. *Revista iberoamericana de educación, 54*(5), 6.

Dominguez, B. M. (2011). Lights and shadows of the measures of attention to diversity in the path of educational inclusion. *Revista Interuniversitaria de Formación del profesorado, 25*(1), 165-183.

Echeverría, B. (2019). *Definition of culture*. Fondo de Cultura Económica.

Ercilla, M. A., & Tejeda, N. B. (1999). Education in values: a pedagogical proposal for vocational training. *University Pedagogy, 4*(3).

Ferrari, J. (2015). New teachers, old schools?

Feldfeber, M. (2007). The regulation of teacher training and work: a critical analysis of the "educational agenda" in Latin America. *Educação & Sociedade, 28*, 444-465.

Freidenberg, F. (2004). The mass media: are they also actors. *Selected Works*, 1-18.

García Aretio, L. (1987). Towards a definition of distance education.

Gómez, I., Ibarra, E., & Areizaga Orube, E. (2005). The cultural component in language teaching as a line of research.

González Lucini, F. (1990). *Education in values and curriculum design*. Madrid: Alhambra Longman, 1990.

Ibáñez-Martín Mellado, J. A. (2006). Religious

freedom and school religious education in an open society. *Bordón: revista de pedagogía.*

Jimenez, M. C., & ESO, P. O. (2009). Critical currents to the traditional school. *Innovation and educational experiences, 14,* 1-9.

Jimenez Martinez, R. (2007). The old school closet. *Advances in educational supervision.*

Martínez Martín, M. (2006). Training for citizenship and higher education. *Ibero-American Journal of Education (OEI), 2006, issue 42, pp. 85-102.*

Martínez, J. L. V., Romero, G. A. F., & Vásquez, D. A. L. (2017). School and family in relation to the extent of academic achievement. The experience of the Antonio José de Sucre Educational Institution of Itagüí (Antioquia) 2015. *Aletheia. Journal of Contemporary Human, Educational and Social Development, 9*(1), 58-75.

Marino, R. A. (2005). Media and education. *Journal of Education, 338,* 85-99.

Marrou, H. I. (2004). *History of Education in Antiquity* (Vol. 80). Akal Editions.

Mendez, R. L. P. (2014). Metaphors and articulations for a critical pedagogy on intersectionality.

Monroy, G. V., & Flores, R. P. (2009). Perspective of human capital theory on the relationship between education and economic development. *Time to Educate, 10*(20), 273-306.

Montenegro Trujillo, A. (2013). Mission of equity and social mobility.

Molina, O. E. (2012). The teacher before the formation of values. Theoretical and practical aspects. *Theory of Education. Education and Culture in the Information Society, 13*(3), 240-267.

Muñoz, F. I., Bartolome, L. I., Sacristán, J. G., Macedo, D., McLaren, P., Popkewitz, T. S., ... & Giroux, H. A. (1999). *Education in the Twenty-first Century: The Challenges of the Immediate Future* (Vol. 136). Graó.

Novo Villaverde, M. (2009). Environmental education, a genuine education for sustainable development. *Journal of Education.*

Lozano, M. C. (1988). Socialisation.

Sauter, G. O. (1993). State and Education in Latin America since its independence (nineteenth and twentieth centuries). *Revista Iberoamericana de educación, 1*.

Cerna Salazar, F. E. (2019). Informative approach and journalistic agenda. A study and analysis of the journalistic coverage of issues related to education in the newspapers La República and El Comercio del Perú.

Sel, S. (2009). Alternative communication and public policies in the Latin American struggle. *Mediatized communication: hegemonies, alternativities, sovereignties, 13-36*.

Maya Nursery, M. S. (2017). *From traditional journalism to that of the millennial generation: Analysis of the transition from the old school to the new formats in digital press* (Bachelor's thesis, Quito).

Ramonet, I. (2013). Media: a power at the service of private interests. *DE MORAES, Denis, RAMONET,*

Ignacio and SERRANO, Pascual. Media, power and counterpower. From monopolistic concentration to the democratization of information. Buenos Aires: Biblos, 47-67.

Ranis, G., & Stewart, F. (2002). Economic growth and human development in Latin America. *ECLAC Magazine.*

Rehaag, I. (2010). The intercultural perspective in education. *The Everyday,* (160), 75-83. Rodriguez, A. B. R. (2010). The fable in primary education. *Pedagogy Magna,* (5), 19-26.

Rotger, A. (1997). *Concept of Social Education* (pp. 9–39). Social Pedagogy.

Rueda, J. L. M., & Fonseca, J. R. (2019). Think about the object of study of school religious education. *Electronic Journal of Religious Education, Didactics and Teacher Training.,* 8(2).

Sanchez, V. M. G. (2009). *Virtual environments for the practical training of education students: implementation, experimentation, and evaluation of the aulaweb platform* (Doctoral dissertation, University of Granada).

Santiago, M. S. (2009). Influence of the Media in Current Education. *http://www. eduinnova. es/ monografias09/medios_comunicacion.pdf.*

Salas, A. L. C. (1997). Economics and Education. *Education Magazine, 21*(1), 99-107.

Schmelkes, S. (2004). Intercultural education: a field in the process of consolidation. *Mexican Journal of Educational Research*, 9(20), 9-13.

Warnier, J. P. (2001). *The globalization of culture.* Editorial Abya Yala.

Zuluaga, C. A. U. (2017). Analysis of the role of the media in the face of scientific dissemination within the framework of Public Policies on Science, Technology, and Innovation. *Notary, 14*(2).

www.ingramcontent.com/pod-product-compliance
Lightning Source LLC
Chambersburg PA
CBHW051746250726
48659CB00001B/265